The Stoplight:
How God's is Operating in Your Life
and
Stoplight Prayers:
Finding the Minutes to be Grateful

Lesa A. McClain

ISBN 978-1-64114-909-9 (paperback)
ISBN 978-1-64114-910-5 (digital)

Christian Faith Publishing, Inc.
832 Park Avenue
Meadville, PA 16335
www.christianfaithpublishing.com

Printed in the United States of America

DEDICATION

This book is dedicated to my granddaughter—Alaina Monaye Giles.
May God light the paths for your feet to follow.

CONTENTS

PRAYER

"Dear God, as we struggle in our busy lives, help us to find time for the joy of communion with you—our Lord and our Maker. Amen" (Carr 2014).

THOUGHT FOR THE DAY

"As we daily communicate with God, we can better see the way God works in our everyday activities" (The Upper Room, July/August 2014, p. 66).

PREFACE

I started out writing this book as a booklet, just a little something to get the thought processes of the people who say that they don't have enough time to pray a little guidance. When I finally got enough courage to submit the manuscript to the publisher (green light), I wondered if I had done the right thing (yellow light). Was it really ready? Was I? Was this what God was leading me to do? Or was this all me? (All yellow-light statements.)

When the call came from the publisher (I let the phone ring a few times), I steadied myself for the bad news. She was going to tell me that my manuscript wasn't good enough. A thank-you-but-no-thank-you kind of scenario played on and on in my head as she talked. All of a sudden, it penetrated into my hard head that she was telling me that I had not been rejected. They liked the concept, but they wanted more. I had written little over five thousand words, and they wanted seven thousand more. *Seven thousand more words!* She might as well have said seven million or seven trillion words! I thanked her and told her that I would work on the manuscript.

My mind shut down. I was recovering from major surgery at the time and as seven thousand more words kept echoing in my head, my mind just shut down. Writer's block, no. Writer's concrete skyscraper, yes. I had no idea where to begin. I talked to one of my friends, and she told me to quit thinking about the amount of words I needed, to just relax, and that my Heavenly Father would guide me along the way. She told me, as I have told so many in the past, "If He brought this to you, He'll see you through it."

I prayed for guidance, and then I let go. I trusted my God, and this book is the results of His labor, through me.

ACKNOWLEDGMENT

Thanks to my daughter, Alisha Giles, to the other three of my big-four support group—Anita and Quan Edgar, and Linda Lewis—for their support. Thanks to everyone who takes the time to read this book. May it be a stepping stone toward building a stronger relationship with God, our Father.

By faith,
Lesa McClain

Defining the Traffic Signal Light (Also Known as the Stoplight)

For the purpose of this inspirational guide, we will refer to the traffic signal light as its better known name, the stoplight.

The stoplight was created in 1912 by Lester Wire, a Detroit, Michigan, policeman; modified in 1920 by another policeman, Walter Potts; and was patented by Garrett Morgan in 1923 (Design Observer). These events occurred long after God had created His world. Man thought that he was just creating a means to move traffic along timely and keep us safe through this directional flow. "That is good," our Father would say because He had another divine purpose in mind when He gave Lester the original idea.

God needed another tool to reach us, and that tool is the stoplight. We know that God is everywhere, but did you ever consider that He would use something as simple as a stoplight to get your attention?

How? Just follow along. Look at the similar meanings for the man's stoplight and God's stoplight.

Man's Stoplight

> **Green** light: Go!
> **Yellow** light: Proceed with caution / prepare to stop.
> **Red** light: Stop!

Each of the colors of man's stoplight has a specific meaning, but *God's* stoplight, even though the colors are the same, has the same and different meanings as they apply to our Father's presence in our lives. Our *God* is a God above all gods and is the master of all the colors of the universe, but for now, we are just going to deal with the colors of the stoplight—the green, the yellow, and the red—the colors we see all day, every day.

God's Stoplight

What could God's **green** light mean?
Green light: Your time has come, go ahead, my child, with my blessing!
Green light: You're doing well! Remember to take time to rest.
Green light: Now go. Think about what I just saved you from.
Green light: This job is yours!

What could God's **yellow** light mean?
Yellow light: Proceed slowly. Makes sure that everything is in line with my Word.
Yellow light: Proceed slowly. Be aware of what is going on around you.
Yellow light: Proceed slowly. There is no need to rush. Everything is on my time, and as you know, I'm never late.
Yellow light: Proceed slowly. You're still healing.
Yellow light: You have a decision to make.
Yellow light: Take time and think.

What could God's **red** light mean?
Red light: Stop! It's not your time yet. Be patient, my child.
Red light: Stop! You need rest.
Red light: Stop! You can't do everything alone. Delegate.
Red light: Stop! I removed him/her from your life for a reason. I have someone that I have selected for you coming your way.

Is this the end of the list? No. This is just a few examples of what God's stoplight could mean because, as we know, we *never* put a limit on what our God can do, nor will we *ever* fully understand His ways. "Such knowledge is too wonderful for me, too lofty for me to attain" (Psalms 139:6, NIV).

Father, Child, and the Stoplight

"…Our Father in heaven…" – Matthew 6:9 NIV.

We are a child of the Most Holy God. He is our Heavenly Father. He is our guide and protector. As our parent, He tries to lead us in the path of righteousness. He picks us up and carries us when we can't carry ourselves.

Carolyn Carty, in 1963, wrote one of three versions of a beautiful poem that reflects how our Father cares for us, a poem that most of us are familiar with, entitled "Footprints."

> *"One night a man had a dream. He dreamed he was walking along the beach with the Lord. Across the dark sky flashed scenes from his life. For each scene, he noticed two sets of footprints in the sand, one belonging to him and one to my Lord.*
>
> *"When the last scene of his life flashed before him, he looked back at the footprints in the sand. He noticed that many times along the path of his life there was only one set of footprints. He also noticed that it happened at the very lowest and saddest times of his life.*
>
> *"This really bothered him, and he questioned the Lord about it. 'Lord, you said once I decided to*

*follow you, you'd would walk with me all the way.
But I have noticed that during the most troublesome
times in my life there is only one set of footprints. I
don't understand why when I needed you most you
would leave me.'*

*"The Lord replied, 'My precious, precious
child, I love you and would never leave you! During
your times of trial and suffering, when you see only
one set of footprints, it was then that I carried you'"*
(*http://www.wowzone.com/fprints.htm*).

Take a look back over your shoulder, and I am sure that you can clearly see how many times He has carried you. Or close your eyes and remember when you thought all was lost, or you couldn't make it another day or you didn't know how you would make it through, but you did. Why? Because He carried you.

Our Father is the light, is of the light, supplies the light, and controls the light. We are children of the light. We have been instructed to let our light shine. We have also been told not to hide our light. Since we are of Him, under His control, God, our Father, is the controller of the stoplight of our lives.

Daily we go about our lives, driving to and from, we stop at the traffic light, sometimes. As we approach the intersection, we look at the light and try to gage the timing to see whether we are going to make it before the light changes to red, making us stop, or whether we should put the pedal to the metal and zip through the yellow light, hoping that if a police car is nearby, the tail end of our car will clear the intersection (allegedly you will not get a ticket for this). Sometimes, in our hurry, especially during the late night or early morning hours, we approach an intersection, look both ways, and proceed through the red light as if it was not meant for us. Sometimes we just do it, but at other times it may actually be for our safety. We're in strange area. People are milling around aimlessly. With tingling awareness (a sign from God as a warning), we go through the light, and once we are moving, we feel relieved. As a side note, if you get stopped by the police, tell them the truth. If they don't believe your story, you will *definitely* get a ticket plus a few points.

How many times have you done a rolling stop? An oxymoron for sure, but people do it all of the time. They come to a stop sign, slow down *almost* to a stop, and then continue on. If you are not guilty of that one, how about this one? You are approaching a stop sign at which you are going to make a right-hand turn. You slow down, again almost stop, and continue your turn. This is a rolling turn. In both incidents, we would argue you down that we had made a full stop before we proceeded on.

Have you done a rolling stop on our Father? How about a rolling turn? I have. In fact one Sunday I did a rolling turn on God. I got dressed for church, left my house, got to church, and because I could not park in my favorite parking lot, I got an instant attitude, made that rolling right turn, circled the block, and headed home. After I was about two blocks from the church, my mind echoed, "You are going home *just because* you couldn't park where you wanted to? You got an attitude about that!"

What would God think about that? Try explaining that to God. "Well, Daddy, I didn't go to church today because when I got there my favorite parking lot was full and I didn't feel like walking from the lot across the street." I could imagine Him responding to me saying something like "You're going to go home because you couldn't park in that one lot? Really? You are going to put off our time together with my other children just because you are lazy? What's next? You go in and can't sit in your favorite seat, you leave?" After that, I believe I would have crawled into the church. I did another rolling turn (I was running late now for church) at the next corner, drove to the church parking lot down and across the street, and parked. As I walked toward the building, I said to myself, "God wanted you to get a little much-needed exercise."

While on the subject of favorite seats, Saints, we ought to get real! Some people sit on the same row every Sunday, but I'm not one of those people who just has to sit there. I have on occasion sat in another row and had other parishioners say to me, "Don't you usually sit over there?" One Sunday I sat on the other side of the church and had a lady ask me to move because I was in her seat. I really and truly don't believe that God wants us to behave this way in His house. Sit somewhere new in the sanctuary. Don't be afraid to move. It will give you another perspective of the pulpit and the sanctuary, and you will meet new people.

Sorry that I had to take that little detour. Every now and then, Daddy will direct me to stop and point out something that He sees as an issue. I'm back on my point about our subject, the stoplight.

Stoplights slow us down. They make us stop when we don't want to. In fact, sometimes we think of them as hindrances to our progress! How many times have you said to yourself, "I would have been on time if I hadn't had to stop at that light"? Stoplights serve their purpose. Think about how different things would be without them? Think of the times that the stoplights have been out of service after a storm. Traffic is backed up. Some people try to stop and let traffic take its turn. Others barrel through. They take their chances. God is like that. He sometimes makes us stop when we don't want to.

We are in constant motion, always adding more and more to our already busy day, barreling through. Eventually, we have a breakdown in health. You get a case of the flu and are home in bed. Even then, you are lying there thinking that you have to be better by tomorrow because you are already behind on so-and-so at work or you were supposed to do this or that instead of getting the rest that you need to recover. God is giving you the time to get the rest that you need but would not take for yourself. God's traffic light says, "**Red** light: Stop! You need rest." Think about this: After you have been sick, when you return back to your everyday life, you don't go all out; you ease yourself back into it. God's traffic light says, "**Yellow** light: Proceed slowly." After a few more days you feel normal again, and God's traffic light says, "**Green** light: You're doing well!" "Remember to take time to rest," God says, "and don't make me stop you again."

CHAPTER 3

The Yellow Light

"Pray that the Lord your God will tell us where we should go and what we should do" (Jeremiah 42:3, NIV).

Can we say *caution*? Can we say *decision*? Can we say that the yellow light is a sign of a cautionary decision? *Caution* is defined as "a warning against danger or evil" (Dictionary.com). *Decision* is defined as "a choice that you make about something after thinking about it" (Merriam-Webster.com).

Another aspect of making a decision is that when you decide to do one thing, you have also decided not to do something else. A decision is always twofold. Here is a simple example: It's 5:00 PM, and you need to go to the cleaner's to get your clothes and go to the post office to pick up a package, and both close at 5:30 PM. After thinking about it, you decide to go to the cleaner's. With that decision, you have decided not to go to the post office, without even saying it. This is why when faced with a decision, we should look closely at the choices and weigh the facts and possible outcomes and pray for guidance.

Man's yellow light cautions us against danger. When the light is changing from green to red, the yellow light between them is to caution us about an upcoming change and that we should give our full attention to the change. Lack of attention to the caution may cause us to be in a car accident resulting in injury or death.

When we approach a traffic light that has just turned yellow, several thoughts that require a decision cross our mind: (1) Will I have enough time to make it through the light? (2) Should I stop? (3) What happens if I go through the light just as it turns red for me and green for the other traffic and there is a car coming that does not have to stop? What do I do? We then decide how we are going to handle the change. Are we going to stop, or are we going to proceed?

Man's yellow light is only relative to you and traffic, but God's yellow light is relevant to your life. God's yellow light not only cautions or warns us against danger, but it also warns us about evil. His yellow light is also a time to make a decision. Just as the yellow light means proceed with caution through the light or make the decision to stop in man's world, it also means proceed with caution in God's world, and it is a pause period that allows us the time to make a decision, to listen to God for direction.

Our Father cautions us against both danger and evil. He tells us that our enemy is not just flesh and blood but also the evil one (Ephesians 6:12). The evil one constantly attempts to control our minds, usually through the weaknesses of the flesh.

Do you know how many cautions there are in the Bible? Do you have any idea how many decisions had to be made in the Bible? Hundreds! Over and over God warns us against things that will cause us harm. Over and over people in the Bible were challenged to make a decision, and because of free will, they didn't always make the right decision, but eventually, they came to the right decision.

Just ask Jonah (in the book of Jonah). God told Jonah to go Nineveh to preach against sin because He had had enough of their wickedness. Jonah ran away from the Lord to Tarshish (that was his way of saying no). To make a short story shorter, Jonah got on a boat, God caused a violent sea storm, they threw Jonah overboard (at his suggestion), and he was swallowed by a whale and spit out on dry land. The Lord again asked Jonah to go to Nineveh, and he went (our God of second chances gave one to Jonah). Jonah could have saved himself a whole lot of grief if he had just obeyed the Lord the first time. Often we don't listen the first time, and when something upsetting or bad happens or when the outcome is not as expected, we fall down on our knees so fast it makes our head spin.

How many times have you said to your children, "Be careful on those stairs, or you might fall and hurt yourself," "Be sure to watch for traffic when you are crossing the street," "Don't talk to strangers," or "Stop running!" These are cautionary statements that prevent harm or danger.

Your Father says the same to you. He just does not vocalize it to you all of the time. Sometimes, He gets other people to say it for Him. How many times has someone told you to "watch your step" because of a trip hazard, or have you walked on stairs that have yellow stripes or are painted yellow on the edge so you can clearly see where the edge of the step is? Or have you seen the Caution: Wet Floor sign? These are all messages from your Father to keep you safe.

When Daddy warns us against something (caution), we don't always heed Him. How many times has He warned you against something and you did it anyway (decision)?

You know that feeling that you get that something is just not right, the doubt, the wind blowing across your neck, causing the hairs on it to stand up? How many times have you said to yourself, "I knew that I shouldn't have done that or gone there. I should have followed my first mind!" Well, the sign or signs that you didn't listen to, which were from Daddy, were His yellow light! He was warning us against harm or danger and we didn't listen.

How about His cautions against the tools of the evil one? Alcohol, drugs, prostitution / sexual promiscuity, gambling, toxic relationships, and so forth, the tools the evil one uses to pry you away from God. Satan tempts us, and because of free will, we sometimes fall into his traps.

At a young age we are introduced to intoxicants. Beer, wine, and liquor were a staple in many households when I was growing up. Marijuana was on just about every corner as I am sure other drugs were there as well. Today, the evils introduced the generation to huffing, which is sniffing aerosols like Freon from air conditioners and the spray for cleaning off computer keyboards. Then bath salts, which they get at their neighborhood store and smoke it, causing them to lose their mind!

Prostitution is still around on the street, and a higher class of prostitutes has been classed up as providing "escort" services. Their customers call, set up an appointment, and off they go.

Because of sexual promiscuity, babies are being born every hour to young girls looking for love in all the wrong places. The bad thing is that as a society, we have accepted this as okay. I've heard, "Well, you know how teens are. That's just what they do," referring to teenagers having sex. I even heard one father say, "I let my boys out and keep my girls in. Ain't no babies coming to my house, but I can't say the same about your house."

Society also wants to blame promiscuity mostly on single-parent homes. I know many, many single parents who have raised their children to be doctors, lawyers, and accountants, without one baby being brought home.

Society also puts single parenting into different categories—those never been married and those divorced."

If you are a never-been-married, then society condemns your children from their birth. They "predict" that your child will grow up to be "nothing but trouble." I have heard that it takes a village to raise a child. Unfortunately, not in this day and age. Try to correct someone's child, and you may find yourself in a fight for your life. *But* if that child grows up to be a God-fearing, positive citizen, then everybody knew that he or she would be "the one."

If you are divorced, society tends to look upon your children in a different way. If they turn out to be horrible human beings, it is all related back to the divorce. The stress of the divorce affected them. It doesn't matter that they were two when the divorce happened. They got their stressors from their parent. If they turn out to be God-fearing, positive citizens, then their parent did a wonderful job *despite* being divorced.

Casinos are popping up everywhere! People drive for miles to the casinos with the hopes of striking it big tonight and sometimes walking away with nothing, not even the rent. I know, personally, where I can find some of my friends on a payday night—the casino.

I really find it interesting when people drive to another part of the state or even to another state to go to a casino. As one of my friends told me, "Change your scenery, change your luck." So far, to my knowledge, that has not worked for him.

Women and even some men are living in toxic relationships. Women are being verbally and physically abused every day by their significant others. Some take the abuse because they have been brainwashed to believe they deserve this treatment because they were bad or they disobeyed. Others stay out of fear. Some have been told that they would be killed if they left, and others are afraid to face the fear of the unknown if they leave, an uncertain future. With every generation, Satan ups his game. He makes the bad look real, real good.

God ups His game, too. In the forefront He has His prayer warriors! They pray in the churches for the communities. In the hardest hit "Satanhoods," you see the warriors on the streets walking or riding in patrols. They are calling out the drug dealers, prostitutes, rapists, and robbers. They are helping to empower the people in the Satanhoods to stand up to crime. God gives them a voice.

He has rehabilitation centers for those who are addicted to alcohol, drugs, sex (Yes, sex! Remember Tiger Woods? He had a sex addiction), and gambling. God has shelters and places of safety for the abused where they can get help and counseling to start a new life. Daddy never said that life would be easy, and He knows how hard it is to resist Satan because His son, Jesus, was tempted (Matthew 4, NIV). He knows that sometimes it takes a long time for His children to realize that they need help before they give in and come to Him. But when you do, He's waiting with open arms.

We can all stand up with Jesus! Prayer warriors, unite! We can fight the good fight of faith.

Daddy also cautions us in other areas. He sends you warning signs about your health. It may start out as a little indigestion that you just take a few antacids and keep moving. Eventually He makes it so bad that you go to see the doctor. They rush you to the hospital. You are having a heart attack! He tried to tell you, but you just wouldn't listen.

Sometimes, He will give you an illness to slow you down. You are running yourself ragged. When you sit down for a few minutes, you drop off to sleep. You are extremely tired, but you keep pushing. Daddy will give you the flu so that you can't go anywhere or do anything. This is His way of cautioning you against something worse. He made the decision for you that you could not make for yourself. He slowed you down.

Our Father wants us to be safe from harm, which is why He cautions us. He knows that Satan is attacking us on all sides, and He is trying to keep us safe. Just listen for His voice.

Talk to God, and He will strengthen you against the attacks of the evil one. Put on His armor (Ephesians 6:10, 6:13–17 NIV) and stand.

C H A P T E R   4

The Red Light

"The way of fools seems right to them, but the wise listen to advice." Proverbs 12:15 NIV

The color red signals danger. It can be physical or financial. We can be red (sunburned or from blushing, usually from embarrassment), we can be in the red (financially, in debt, owing money), or we can see red (be very angry or enraged). Whether you are red, in the red, or seeing red, red is not a good condition to be in, so when God's red light comes on, you'd better *stop*!

Ever notice at the end of the summer how much darker your left arm is compared to your right arm from driving your car during the summer? For most of us this is called tanning, but for some, their skin turns red, burns, and may blister. This is called sunburn. Most people that burn easily are on the watch for the telltale sign of their skin turning red. Being alert stops them from the pain and anguish that comes with sunburn.

How about the time when that very cute girl or handsome guy that you have a crush on spoke to you and later when someone mentioned that they saw you talking to so-and-so, you felt warmth come into your cheeks? That's called blushing. It is an increase of blood to your face, causing your cheeks to color red. This is mostly caused by embarrassment. In this case, when someone knows that you have a crush on someone, they will pleasantly tease you about it and cause the blushing. It fades away almost as fast as it came. Think about this: In cosmetics, the powder or crème that we women put on our cheeks is called—what?—blush! God probably looks at this and laughs. He loves to see His children smitten. He wants nothing but the best for you.

There may be have been a time in your life or in the life of someone you know when their debts exceeded their income, meaning that they owed more than they earned. This could be credit card debt or just the daily living expenses. Some of us just love to shop! We *needed* that purse, hat, dress, shoes, or whatever. We just had to have it! Now your credit card is maxed out, and all you can pay is the minimum. Now on credit card statements, they have a little box that tells you how long it is going to take for you to pay that off when you just pay the minimum. Depending on the amount owed, it could take *years* to pay it off!

Guess what happened now? The refrigerator died! What are you going to do? Go to the appliance store and—yep—open a credit account. You can get the refrigerator with all of the bells and whistles that you always wanted. You decide you might as well look at the washers and dryers too because yours is kind of old, and since they gave you this wonderful line of credit, why not? Look, there is that top-of-the-line washer and dryer you've been dying to have! Might as well get that set right there. You walk out of the store smiling, not even bothered by the fact that you have just spent five thousand dollars on appliances thinking (1) you deserved it and (2) so-and-so is going to be jealous. You just spent five thousand dollars that you didn't have in the first place, and you are actually happy about it—until the bill comes. The cycle goes on and on.

How many times has Daddy tried to stop you from reckless spending? Credit card at the limit? Stop. Can't find your credit card? Stop. You were delayed in getting to the store, and it had just closed when you pulled up for the one-day sale? Stop. Misplaced your keys that miraculously appeared after the stores closed? Stop.

Daddy tried to convince you that you didn't need to buy a house with four bedrooms and three baths, a house that was far too expensive for your financial status. It was only you, your husband, and the dog! But you wouldn't listen to Him. He threw a low credit score. Stop. You had to up get more money out of your pension because the down payment is higher. You owed the IRS six thousand dollars for all those years that you owed taxes and had made arrangements for. Now you have to pay that off in order for the deal to go through. That was another stop, but you just went and got more money out of the pension fund. You still have twenty years left to work; that's plenty of time to rebuild the fund. You kept at it until you got this house, and when all was done, you were happy because it was bigger that your sister's house. (Be sure to read the red-light rules that follow. This is number 10.) Now your old furniture doesn't go with the new house, and on and on.

If you own your own home, you may have an adjustable mortgage. Very rarely have I seen a mortgage adjust down, and sometimes, an additional twenty or thirty dollars can put a strain on an already tight budget.

Here in the northern states, we cringe at the thought of winter coming. With the cold weather comes high heating bills and which sometimes exceed what you can afford to pay. You get on the budget plan, in which they estimate how much you should pay every month of the year. They base this payment on the total amount that you are billed the year before. This amount may be high, but you know how much it is going to be every month. And trust me, it is really hard to pay $200 in June when your actual bill for June would be $30 dollars because your mind has closed itself to the fact that in December your bill was $310. In February, they reassess the bill, and most of the time you have a balance that your monthly payments didn't cover because you decided that you were on the budget plan anyway so you crank that thermostat up! Guess what. Now you have a balloon payment due for the amount that your monthly payments didn't cover. Guess what else. You don't have the additional money. So they recalculate your bill, and now your new payment is even higher!

Daddy just shakes His head. "You, my child, are in trouble, in the red, just because you just didn't stop when I tried to help you." You eventually turn to Daddy for help, and that help may be in the form of a second job.

Just to put a little humor to our financial woes is a joke that Joel Osteen told one Sunday morning:

> *"A man is talking to God, 'God how long is a million years?'*
> *"God answers, 'To me, it's about a minute.'*
> *"'God, how much is a million dollars?'*
> *"'To me, it's a penny,' God replied.*
> *"'God, may I have a penny?'*
> *"'Wait a minute'" (https://uinjokes.com/joke-5580/).*

Let's look at a couple of red-light situations from the Bible that had adverse outcomes. The first one is Sodom and Gomorrah (Genesis 19:1–25). I don't think the light could have gotten any redder! The two angels that the Lord had sent to destroy the cities offered to spare Lot and all the people whom he was related to. You know how people are. I can hear them saying, "Lot's crazy! I'm not leaving my stuff!" "Man, go on with that crazy talk. Ain't nobody said nothing about no fire."

In the end, the angels took Lot, his wife, and his two daughters, escorted them outside of the city, sending them on their way with the admonition "Don't [another word for *stop*] look back" among many other cautions. When they had reached the city where they would be safe, Lot's wife (I can hear her thinking, "What is one little peek going do?") turned and looked back, and we know what happened to her. She turned into a pillar of salt. Apparently Lot and his daughters heeded the warning because you don't read about them turning into pillars salt (Genesis 19:26). I can imagine Lot looking at his wife through eyes of love, saying, "I can't leave her." They probably loaded her carefully into the cart and took her to their new home, giving her a place of honor in the kitchen. I can almost hear Lot saying to his daughters one night after they had finished cooking and sat down to dinner, "Hey, this needs a little flavor. Go get a few chips off of your mother."

The second one is about the Ark of the Covenant, a story in which someone thought that they were saving the Ark and it cost him his life. Aaron and his son had been given strict instructions on preparing the holy articles and furnishings for travel any time they moved the camp with the Ark of the Covenant (also known as Ark of God or the Ark of Testimony). After Aaron and his sons had finished covering the holy furnishings and all the holy articles, they called the Kohathites, whose responsibility was to take care of the most holy things in the Tent of Meeting. Whenever the camp was ready to move, the Kohathites were called to come and carry the most holy items. They were admonished not to touch the holy things or they would die (Numbers 4:15).

When the Kohathites came to the threshing floor of Nakon, Uzzah, a Kohathite, reached out and took hold of the Ark of God because the oxen had stumbled and he did not want it to fall. The Lord's anger burned against Uzzah because of his irreverent act—the touching of the most important holy thing after being warned not to touch any of the most holy things. Therefore God struck him down, and he died there beside the Ark of God (2 Samuel 6:6–7).

Here was a man who thought that he was doing a good thing, and I am sure that when the oxen stumbled, he reacted and probably had not even thought of the warning. We react to a lot of things. For example, you are sitting at the dining room table, and someone accidently knocks a glass over. The glass is rolling toward the edge of the table. You try to catch the glass before it rolls off the table because you know it will surely break. The glass breaking causes shards of glass going everywhere, someone getting cut trying to pick them up, and the like, so you try to react. You try to catch it; you don't want the glass to fall. That's all Uzzah did was react, but his reaction caused him his life.

When you are doing something and it is not working out right, God is probably trying to gently stop you from doing whatever it is. He is probably trying to stop you from reaching out, trying to keep the Ark from falling, and keeping you alive. You never know.

Ever have one of those feelings and you listen to it and later find out that something negative happened? I had one not too long ago coming home from work. It was a Thursday, and I was going to stop at the bank. As I pulled into the parking lot, a voice said, "You can do this tomorrow [Stop]." So I left the bank, and later on the six-o'clock news I found out that the same branch of the bank that I was at was robbed that afternoon. The time they gave for the robbery was approximately 3:55 PM. I pulled out of the bank lot at 3:50 PM. Even though no one was hurt, I would have been in the bank when the robbery occurred.

The voice that I heard was the voice of God, stopping me, and you can't convince me otherwise! You will never know how many prayers of thanks I gave him that night! I also sent up a prayer thanking Him for protecting those who were in the bank at that time. This is just one example from our Father letting us know that He has our interest at heart.

God gives us additional stops or red-light moments for our good throughout His Word. Many, many times He asks us or tells us to "be still." That is His way of telling us to stop. One of my favorites is

"Be still and know that I am God…" Psalms 46:10 NIV.

God wants us to stop and listen to His voice. He wants us to know His voice. He wants us to just stop and listen to the birds singing their sweet melodies, the songs that He gave them, listen to the wind rustling through the trees, the babbling of a brook, the laughter of a child. These are just some of the things that He gave as a gift to us to reach that peaceful place within us. Be still and enjoy what He has done for you. It is His symphony of love.

Other times He wants us to put our fears and worries aside and rely on our faith in Him. In Isaiah 43:5 NIV, God tells us to reassure us, "Don't be afraid for I am with you…" He lets us know that He is always with us. "Stop worrying, have no fear, for I am here." Believe in Him. Trust in Him.

In addition to Daddy telling us to listen to His voice and putting our fears aside, He needs us to know that He will fight for us. Exodus 14:14 says, "The Lord will fight for you; you need only to be still." A better known verse in the Bible is 2 Chronicles 20:15 NIV: "…For the battle is not yours, but God's." Take heed of His Word.

He is armed for a battle that you could never win alone. We have a *big* God who is capable of handling all of our little problems.

"Quiet," Jesus said to the storm as the boat was being tossed around in the ocean. The disciples had been afraid that the boat was going to capsize in the storm, and they went and awakened Jesus. Jesus spoke to the storm and calmed the sea. "What kind of man is this? Even the wind and the waves obey Him!" the disciples said to one another (Matthew 8:23–27). "Is he truly the Savior?"

Yes, He is. The Jesus that calmed the seas is the same Jesus that calms the seas of our life, if we ask Him. He knows what is happening in our lives, but He just wants us to talk to Him about it and invite Him in to our lives, and He will calm all of the storms in our lives.

CHAPTER 5

God's Red-Light Rules

"You shall not..." Exodus 20:3 NIV.

Just as our earthly parents gave us rules to live by – such as no hitting, no biting, no shoving your little sister, and others like mind your manners, no dating until you are sixteen (or thirty-five, as some of us parents would prefer), and be home by midnight (The list goes on and on, but your parents just wanted you to turn out to be a benefit to society and to be safe) – God is the same way. God created a list of red-lights rules for our benefit. High upon Mount Sinai, God etched the rules to live by on stone tablets and gave them to Moses. His original list of stops is called the Ten Commandments. For your viewing pleasure, they can be found in His Word: Exodus 20:3–17 NIV.

The rules are as follows, with a little clarification (in parentheses). By no means am I trying to translate God's thoughts for Him. I just made them simpler so that I could understand them, and I decided to share.

The 10 Commandments (God's Red-Light Rules)

1. *You shall have no other gods before me.* (Do not worship any other gods, for I am your one and only God. Think about this one: You are involved in a car accident. The first thing that comes out of people's mouth, not all people and gen-

erally not this nicely, is "You hit my car!" or "See what you did to my car!" Not "Are you okay?" Replace the word *car* with *god*. See my drift here?)

2. *You shall not make for yourself an idol in the form of anything in the heaven above or on the earth beneath or in the waters below.* (Do not worship birds, dog, fish, etc., but do enjoy them, for they are a gift from God. Let me go a little further, have you heard of sun worshippers? These were people who, in ancient Egypt, actually worshipped the sun god Ra. Sun worshippers of today are just ordinary people lying out in the sun, getting tanned.)

3. *You shall not misuse the name of the Lord in vain.* (I don't have to remind you saints about using the Lord's name in one of your un-Christian-like conversations. You all know what I'm talking about. Remember, "out of the same mouth come praise and cursing. My brothers and sisters, this should not be. Can both freshwater and salt water flow from the same spring?" [James 3:10–11, NIV].)

4. *Remember the Sabbath day by keeping it holy.* (Whatever day is your Sabbath, you should keep it holy. God instructed us to rest and relax on this day because He gave us six other days to work and toil, but I am, as many of you, guilty of doing many things on the Sabbath. Does laundry, grocery shopping, or cleaning the house ring a bell? I am guilty as charged, but I am working to get back to what God commands me to do on the Sabbath, and that is to rest.)

5. *Honor your father and mother…* (Respect you parents. They are the vessel that God used to bring you here to Him. Not all parents are ideal, and some people may not have two parents or even know who their parents are, but honor them for assisting God in getting you here to Him. If they are still alive, go and thank them for giving you safe passage. Honor them with your words and deeds. Those of you that harbor ill will against your father or mother, thank God for them. You are not perfect, and neither are they. Whatever it is that you are holding against them is actually

hurting you more than it is hurting them. I had a friend who harbored a lot of hurt feelings toward her mother. When she finally got around to expressing her feelings and anger to her mother, who was in failing health, her mother didn't remember. I could actually say that my friend was hurt even more because she had carried this pain around for most of her life. Even if they have passed on, let the hurt and pain go. God can help you. Ask God to soften your heart so that you can be open to forgive your parent or parents and move on with your life.)

6. *You shall not commit murder.* (This is very clear. Remember Cain and Abel? Cain, a fieldworker, was the older of the first two of Adam and Eve's children. Abel attended the flocks. In time, Cain brought some of the fruit as an offering to the Lord. Abel also brought offering, fat portions of meat from the firstborn of his flock. The Lord look with favor on Abel and his offering, but He did not look as favorable on Cain and his offering, so Cain got angry. Cain and Abel went to the field where Cain killed his brother. To make a long story short, Cain was banished to the land of Nod by God for killing his brother [Genesis 4, NIV]. [On a much smaller note but to admit my transgression, let me pray for the spider I just killed. It was in self-defense. I knew he was coming for me!])

7. *You shall not commit adultery.* (I should not have to explain this one, but here goes. If you are married, the only person that you date and have intimate relationship with is your spouse. If you are mad at your husband or wife, you don't call one of your exes to chat. Even if you don't participate in any activities with your ex, you may have committed adultery in your heart. This is just my opinion, and I'm entitled to it. Today, Facebook is listed as one of the top reasons why people get divorced. Husbands and wives are going on Facebook wondering about their exes. The next thing you know, they have contacted that person, they get to talking and wondering what if, and the story ends in a

divorce or two. I'm not saying that this happens all of the time, but it is happening far too often.)

8. *You shall not steal.* (We are all guilty of this some time or another. If you don't believe me, that pen or pencil that you are writing with had to come from somewhere. If you didn't by it, I rest my case. Stealing is stealing. How about that extra fifteen minutes you took for lunch or that thirty to forty minutes you spent chatting with a coworker before going back to work? Didn't you just steal some time out of your work day, paid time? Here is another one that I didn't think about until someone pointed it out to me. You are in the grocery store, and you are thinking about getting some grapes or cherries. You pop a couple in your mouth to see if they are sweet. If they are, you buy them. If not, you move on. Let your conscience decide if this is stealing or not. Just remember, you didn't pay for the ones you ate. God said don't do it; stealing is wrong.)

9. *You shall not give false testimony against your neighbor.* (Who is your neighbor? Anyone you come in contact with. Stop lying to people! If someone asked you whether you saw an event occur and you didn't, just say no and move on. I can't tell you how many times I've watched the news and a person is telling the reporter, "He looked like he did something." People have been known to lie about another person just because they don't like them. People, you are wrong. If you can't prove it, don't say it. Just don't lie about anyone.

10. *You shall not covet you neighbor's house, his wife, his servant, his donkey or anything that belongs to your neighbor* (paraphrased). (Stop hating, people! Stop wishing you had his house or wishing your wife or husband was as good looking as so-and-so's, wishing you had a new car, better clothes like so-and-so! You don't know what they sacrificed to get what they have. Even though the grass looks greener on the other side of the fence, upon a closer look it may be

crabgrass! Stop wanting what others have and do what you have to do to get what you desire.)

In summation, there is no little cussing, no little murder, no little adultery, no "I just took one, they will never miss it," and no little white lies. These are all sins, and there is no little sin, and we all are guilty of some of them at some time. Before you accuse your sister or brother in Christ, remember to remove the "plank" from your own eye (Luke 6:42, NIV), or if you are without sin, be the first to cast the stone (John 8:7 NIV).

The list of the Ten Commandments is the only one that most people know about, but God gave us more. To read other rules to live by—or as I call them, "The Stops, Part 2"—read Exodus chapter 21.

CHAPTER 6

The Green Light

"Whoever gives heed to instruction prospers and blessed is he who trusts in the Lord" (Proverbs 16:20, NIV).

Over and over throughout our lives we have green-light moments. Remember when you applied for a job that you had doubts that you would get? You were sure that someone else more qualified had applied, but *something* made you go ahead and apply. Remember how you felt when you got the call to come in for the interview? Remember that call that said that you got the job and when could you start? That something that made you go ahead and apply was one of your Daddy's green-light moments! He knew that this job would be perfect for you.

You have been married for six years. You and your husband have been trying to have a child for three years, but to no avail. You and your husband both work fifty to sixty hours a week to get ahead. You are in school working on your master's degree. Two years ago you bought a nice house, and you both drive nice cars, but the one thing that is missing is a child. A year ago, you finished your degree; at the same time your job goes through a restructuring. You are laid off.

Your husband is reassigned to another position, forty hours with a 10 percent pay cut. Armed with your degree, you apply for and get a new position making 25 percent more, working forty hours. You know that things are going to be okay. It's almost as if nothing has changed. On the day of the one-year anniversary of your new job, you find out that you are pregnant! You see, your Daddy aligned everything in your favor so that you could enjoy your baby. He gave you a green light.

There are so many green-light moments in our lives! You go to a little league baseball game to watch your nephew play. You really didn't want to go, but because you nephew asked you, you went (green light). The guy sitting next to you strikes up a conversation with you. That game was two years ago. You are marrying that guy, your soul mate, next month.

You are laid off from work. You are getting assistance from the state, but it is not enough, but you are thankful for what you get. You go to church, and you put in your tithes. They take up a collection to help some families in the church. You put your last two dollars (green light) in the collection plate, hoping that little bit will help. On Tuesday, your doorbell rings. It's one of the ministers from the church. She hands you a check for five hundred dollars! You find out you were one of the families they were collecting for! God blessed you more than 250-fold!

You are sick. You are itching all over. It's not all of the time, just sometimes. The doctors have given you an antihistamine, and it works when you take it when the itching starts, but they can't find the source. On your next office visit, your regular nurse is out sick, so you get a new nurse (green light). You start talking, and you are telling her about the itching. She looks at your chart and says that she sees that you take Motrin for knee pain, and asks if you have ever taken half a pill. You say yes. She asks if it had a thin paper coating. You say yes. When the doctor comes in, she tells him that you may be allergic to the coating on the Motrin. She knows because she has the same problem. The doctor tells you to take the antihistamine pill with the Motrin next time you take it. Guess what, no more itching!

Take a minute to think about your life. Search out the green lights. Anytime God gives us the go-ahead, no matter what the situation is, it's His green light.

CHAPTER 7

Be Grateful

"Give thanks to the Lord, call on his name; make known among the nations what he has done" (1 Chronicles 16:8, NIV).

Most of us, including me, are not grateful for all that our Father does for us. We grumble and complain, and in fact, some of us have a very bad case of keeping up with the Joneses! And trust me, the Joneses don't just live next door.

How many times have you said to yourself, "I wish I had a house like so-and-so" or "I wish I had a relationship like she has with her children" or even "I wish I had her hair." I wish, I wish, I *wish*! Do you realize that you are breaking a commandment? *Thou shalt not covet* (Exodus 20:17, NIV)! (Go back to chapter 5 and refresh yourself with Stop 10!)

We want whatever someone else has that *seems* better than what we have—a better car, more money, better kids, better relationships, better hair. You want a better, car but are you willing to pay a "better" car note? You want more money, and yes, we would all like to hit the lottery, but are you willing to do what it takes—additional training, more education to get a better job—to be able to make more? Better kids? You raised those heathens! Okay, okay, we are not 100 percent responsible for how our kids turn out. They fall into a bad crowd, etc., and no matter what we do, they get into trouble. Or we gave them too much—to many toys to make up for what we perceived to be a lack in our lives (I never had a lot of toys or I didn't have a TV in my room because we couldn't afford it), too much freedom (my parents were strict, and we had to be in by 11:00 PM on the weekends, so as long as my kids keep up good grades, I will cut them a little slack). You want a better relationship? You have to give better to get better. Better hair? You have to deal with what our Father gave you or buy some! You can buy long, short, straight, kinky, wavy, blonde, red, purple, whatever. Whatever will make you happy for those few moments in time, *because* when it is all said and done, you still have your God-given locks. They have not changed and are still yours. You can press, perm, or dye, but you will always come back to the fact that you have curly or kinky or straight or wavy hair.

Whatever we so desire, our Father wants to give it to us. He wants to bless us beyond compare, if we ask, but—and yes, there is a *but*—if we are not good stewards of what He has given us, then explain to me, why He should give us more.

Does this sound like you? "Lord, I really would like another house. One just a little larger." Well, let me tell you, girlfriend, there is so much dust on the furniture that you have now the tops look white. Now, if you can't keep this smaller house clean, why would He give you a larger one?

Or "Lord, I am waiting for you to send me the man/woman that you have for me." Are you still kicking it with your old one? God told you a long time ago that he/she was no good, but you still have him/her around. So why is He going to send you the one He has for you? Apparently, no matter what God has said, you have decided that any man/woman is better than no man/woman and that despite what you ask for or what you are destined to have, maybe you better hold on to what you have, hoping that God will eventually change him/her into the man/woman you want him/her to be.

It isn't going to happen that way. What God has for you is for you, so you need to let go and let God bless you in His own divine way.

Trust Daddy. Work on your relationship with Him. Commit yourself to loving Him unconditionally. Remember, He gave His son's life for yours, which should tell you how much He loves you. He will provide all of your needs and some of your wants, in His time. Just wait for Him.

CHAPTER 8

The Ultimate Red and Green Light

"…so the son of man must be lifted up, that every-one who believes may have eternal life in him." –
John 3:14-15 NIV.

God, our Father, used the ultimate **red** light for His Son, our brother, Jesus Christ. John 3:16 (NIV) says: "For God so loved the world that He gave His one and only Son so that whoever believes in Him shall not perish but have eternal life." What a wonderful gift! Jesus was God's ultimate **green** light.

Jesus. Jesus. Read what they did to my Lord, then close your eyes and picture it:

We all know the story of the Crucifixion, but do we really think about the times leading up to the Crucifixion? Jesus was tried, mocked, and beaten before He made it to the cross on Calvary. When I say beaten, most people think that it was just an ordinary whip, but Jesus was no ordinary man. And He was not just beaten, but He was stripped and scourged with an extraordinary whip called a flagrum or a flagellum.

A flagrum was whip with several tongs or strands up to three feet long with weighted lead balls, at least two, and sometime three pieces of bone on each strand. The flagrum was designed to lacerate the skin. Each blow to my Savior's back cut it open. Some say that He received forty lashes, and others say four hundred, but however many there were, my God bore a weight that only a man born of God could bear and still hang on the cross for us. Witnesses to other flagrum beatings say that they saw the innermost parts of some the flogees bodies, even to the bowels (*Truth Magazine* Jan. 2000). This what Jesus endured for us!

After He was beaten, He was tasked to carry His cross to the top of the mount. A man was tasked to help Him to carry His cross. Why? The beating had left Him unable to make the journey. When He was placed on the cross, I can't believe that He was gently placed on a polished piece of wood but rather roughly thrown down on a piece of rough wood and nailed to the cross. Did my Lord cry out as they nailed Him to the cross? Or was He in so much pain that He never really distinguished it from the rest of His pain. We will never know, because there is no mention of it in the Bible.

When they lifted the cross with His pain-wracked body, can you imagine Him sliding down the rough wood of the cross, tearing His skin, splintering His body? Can you see the holes in His hands tearing larger as His weight pulled on them? Can you see the pain that God went through seeing His son dying for us? Can you see it? Can you see what God did for us? Can you see it?

There were many stoplight moments in Jesus's life, but when He hung on the cross on Calvary, dying for our sins (**red** light), so that we could live (**green** light), He became God's **ultimate** light.

C H A P T E R   9

Stoplight Stories—Yesterday, Today, and Forever

"Jesus Christ, the same, yesterday and today and for-ever" (Hebrews 13:8 NIV).

Yesterday's stoplight stories are stories that illustrate how God used the stoplight principle long before the stoplight was invented. There are quite a few stories in the Bible. Remember Mary's stories? She became with child (green light). When she told Joseph, he decided to leave her. An angel stopped (red light) Joseph from leaving. Mary went into labor (yellow light) while they were traveling. There was no room for them at the inn (red light). Nothing but the barn, the place where our Savior was born (green light) (Luke 2:1–7).

What about Noah building the ark (green light) even when everyone thought that he had lost his mind (Genesis 6:14–22)? (For a mind-boggling experience, go visit Williamston, Kentucky, or go online to arkencounter.com to see a full-size replica of the ark that Noah built.)

One of my favorite stories is the one about the three Hebrew boys thrown into the fiery furnace because they would not bow down and worship the golden image that Nebuchadnezzar had had made. It became extremely special when I came across this verse in the Bible: "…When you walk through the fire, you will not be burned;

the flames will not set you ablaze." (Isaiah 43:2 NIV) Now, I believe that the Bible was written in the order in which events occurred, which means, correct me if I'm wrong, that God made this promise before the Hebrew boys went into the furnace.

They walked into the furnace (green light) believing that the God that they served would stop (red light) any harm that they would encounter, including fire. Not only did He save them (green light), but He walked in the furnace with them, and I can only imagine the conversation (Daniel 3:1–28, NIV)!

Even today, God still imparts His wisdom when we are lacking our own. Everything that you have belongs to Him. It is just on loan to you. You are a steward over the things He has given you to use. He can take it all away at a moment's notice. Ask people who have lived through a fire or a natural disaster, and they will tell you that things can be here today and gone tomorrow. Sometimes you will hear someone say, "God is good! I've got my health and my strength, and my family is okay. We can start over." Some will bemoan their stuff. I understand this, but I have found out that those who scream the loudest have a tendency to have the least faith. Just like with Job, He can restore it all and with even more than you can imagine.

Our forevers are all resting comfortably in Daddy's hands. Daily He checks His schedule to see what He has planned for us. It could be a blessing or a lesson. We never know about His day-to-day plans for our life, but what we do know is that one day Daddy will call us home. Daddy will use His green light to bring us home to Him, His beacon of direction. In our eyes, it will appear as a white light showing us the pathway to our new life.

His Word says when He sees that you have fought the good fight of faith (2 Timothy 4:7–8) and He knows that you are weary, He stretches out His hand and says, "Come to me and I will give you rest" (Matthew 11:28), and He takes us home. Even though He knows that the love ones we leave behind will miss us, He no longer wants to see His child suffer, so He brings us home to Him, where we shed the old body and put on the new one, one that has no pain, no worries, one that is free.

There have been times in my life that I have seen people turn away from God because they had prayed for their loved one to be healed and their loved one had died. I have held their hands while they lamented, "He said in His Word that if I asked, I would be given the desires of my heart. I asked, I begged, and my momma still died! Why did He let her die?" I had no answer to help with their pain. I began to have questions myself. Was God not answering the prayers of the righteous because of something we had done on our part, or was there some other reason?

I asked a minister who I had a wonderful relationship with. He looked heavenward and seemed to be in deep thought as to how he was going to answer me. He looked at me and said, "The prayers of the righteous did not fail. When we are praying for someone to be healed and they go home to be with the Lord, we never even consider what they may be praying for. We are praying for them to stay, and they are praying to go be with the Lord. So instead of praying for them to get well, we should pray for God's will in their life." Over the years, I have passed this on to others, and it always seemed to help.

Sometimes, you have to realize and respect what God is doing in your life. When things happen, we often wonder why—why this, why that, "why does this happen to me"? God *never* promised that your life would be a stroll in the park. He tells us that there a consequences to disobeying His Word, and what do we do? Disobey! Even in His Word He refers to us as "stubborn and hard-headed people" (Acts 7:51 CEV), which we are. We are quick to blame others for our problems. Remember Adam? "That woman that you made for me made me do it" (Genesis 3:12). Eve was saying, "The serpent made me do it" (Genesis 3:13).

When the tempter tempted, he did harm to all of us. The first bite of the fruit from the tree of the knowledge of good and evil gave us free will and, unfortunately for us females, labor pains!

Our Father actually saves us from ourselves, most of the time. He delays us, He detours us, He removes people from our lives who mean us no good, and on the other hand, He blesses us with all of the things that we need because He is our supply (Philippians 4:19). He is a wonderful and loving parent, but just like our earthly parents,

He does not "spare the rod" (Proverbs 13:24). He punishes us for our own good. We may not see it that way, but He knows what's best for us. Our limited vision for our life is no match for His forever vision of our lives.

CHAPTER 10

What Are Stoplight Prayers?

"And pray in the Spirit on all occasions with all kinds of prayers and request..." (Ephesians 6:18 NIV).

Stoplight prayers are exactly that, prayers that you say when you have stopped in traffic for the stoplight. We, the children of the risen Lord, are quick to say that we just don't have the time to pray. According to Francois Fenelon, a French Roman Catholic archbishop,

"Tell God all that is in your heart, its pleasures and its pains, to a dear friend. Tell God your troubles, that God may comfort you: tell God your joys, that God may sober them; tell God your longings, that God may purify them; tell God your dislikes, that God may help you conquer them; talk to God of your temptations, that God may shield you from them; show God the wounds of your heart, that God may heal them. If you thus poor out all your weaknesses, needs, troubles, there will be no lack of what to say. Talk out of the abundance of the heart, without consideration say just what you think. Blessed

are they who attain to such familiar, unreserved intercourse with God."

That is exactly what prayer is—a conversation with God. If you said a prayer at every stoplight or even every other stoplight, do you realize how many prayers, acts of gratitude, intercessory prayers you could pray in the course of one day?

Stoplight prayers are just the catalyst for small periods of prayer. There are many, many times during the day that you can pray. Think about this: You are sitting at your desk, silently saying grace over the food that you are about to eat. (You do say grace over your meals, right?) Would it really take a whole lot of time to add to your prayer and ask the Lord to bless so-and-so who is going through a hard time?

Silent prayer can be done anywhere at any time. Your prayers don't have to be long, drawn-out, ten-minute vocal sessions; they can be short, sweet, silent, and from the heart.

You say that you don't have a lot of time for prayer? It is amazing what we do have time for. We go to the grocery store. That's right. You have to go there. You have to eat. Have you thought about thanking God for the car that is taking you to the grocery store? How about the money for the groceries? How about thanking Him for the strength and the ability to walk around in the store? If everybody could walk around the store on their own, then the stores would not have those electric riding carts. Think about that!

How many times have you stopped at a light and reached over and checked your cell phone for a message? Or called someone? Or changed a CD? Or plugged your smartphone into the car to listen to your favorite playlist? Or mentally gone over the list of things that you still have to do before you go to bed that night?

How about having a little talk with Jesus? Think of all of the minutes that you ride in your car listening to music. You can cut the music down a little and talk to your Daddy. Daddy likes music, too. That's why we sing hymns of praise. He'd love to hear from you! You don't need a specific form of prayer; just talk to Him. That's all; just start talking. You don't even have to call His name; He will know that you are talking to Him.

Talk to Him like He is your best friend, your BFF, which He should be. What do you talk to Him about? Anything, everything. Start with stoplight prayers. When you stop at a red light, make a point of talking to Daddy. At each light, you can thank Him for something that you are grateful for. At one stoplight, you can tell Him about a problem; at another, be an intercessor for someone.

I was doing a form of intercessory prayer and didn't even know it until a minister pointed it out to me. You see, I collect seashells and pretty rocks. People will bring me shells back from their vacations. A few years ago, I read that sometimes, when a person is really going through a difficult time, they need something to bring the good and wonderful things in their life back to their minds, back to focus, so I started giving a seashell or a pretty rock to them. I tell them that neither the seashell nor the rock has special powers, that if they happen to lose it, it's okay. It's only a shell or a rock, but its purpose right now is to be constant reminder of all that is good and wonderful things in their lives. I ask them to carry it with them, like in their pants pocket, or place it somewhere that they will see it several times a day and when they touch it or see it, think about something good in their lives.

Most of these people, I don't know. They may be the spouse of a coworker or a friend of a friend. I generally carry a shell or a rock for myself, and there have been times that a conversation has occurred while I'm in the grocery store line and I've given up my rock or shell. I've had people come back and tell me that they thought it was a dumb idea when I gave them the shell or rock for a loved one, but once they saw how it affected their love one, they were glad that I had given them the shell or the rock. You can never know how something as small as a shell or a rock can have such significant impact on someone by redirecting their focus.

Here are a few examples of types of prayers just to get you started on your way:

When I wake up in the morning:
- *Thank You, Jesus,* for waking me up this morning, allowing me to see another day!

- Thank You for waking me up in my right mind.
- Thank You that my body is functioning as You designed it.
- I even thank You for any pain that I am feeling or any illness that I have because I am alive to fight it another day.
- I am thankful that I am able to shower and dress without any help.

As I leave for work in the morning:
- Daddy, thank You for seeing me safely to my car. (You never know. There could have been someone waiting in the bush for their next victim, who could have been you. God distracted them, and you made it safely to your car and drove away.)
- Thank You for this car.
- Daddy, lead my way safely with traveling mercies to the job that You gave me.

I see a car on the side of the road with the flashers on:
- Thank You for guiding them safely on to the shoulder of the road without harm.

I see an accident without apparent injuries:
- Lord, even though there was a fender bender, everyone looks okay.

I see an accident with apparent injuries:
- Daddy, cover them with Your healing mercies.
- Bless the healthcare workers who will be assisting the injured.

When I get to work:
- Thank You for bringing me safely to this job that You have blessed me with.

Other times (at stoplights):
- Thank You for blessing me with life.

- Thank You for this day.
- Thank You for continuing to bless me.
- Thank You for allowing me to be a blessing to someone.
- Thank You for my husband/wife/kids/girlfriend/boyfriend.
- Thank You for my family and friends.
- Thank You for giving me the opportunity to give a kind word to someone who really needs it.
- Thank You for allowing me to give and receive hugs.
- Thank You for the roof over my head, the heat to keep me warm, the lights that remove the dark, and the food in my refrigerator for my nourishment.
- So-and-so is going through something. Give him/her the strength to continue through and come out victorious on the other side.
- Satan's been busy in my life today. Give me the strength to overcome.
- My knee hurts a little today, but I am grateful that I can feel the pain, because some people don't have a knee or a leg. I am truly blessed.
- Thank You for blessing that person in the wheelchair, that when he/she could have felt sorry for themselves, they didn't let their disability get them down.
- Thank You for holding all those who are grieving in Your everlasting arms.
- Thank You for blessing the expectant mothers with health as they await the gift that You have given them.
- Thank You for the gift of love and the ability to give it freely.
- Continue to teach me to let go adopting the "Let God" principle and let You handle the problems.

These are just a few examples, but you know your story, and you know what you are thankful for.

I bet you won't look at a stoplight the same way ever again. Pass it on. There can never too many people thanking God for what He has done or sending up prayers for those who need them.

Be blessed and be a blessing!

BIBLIOGRAPHY

Carr, Marietta. 2014. "Daily Tasks." *The Upper Room* (July/August): 66.

Carty, Caroline. "Footprints." http://www.wowzone/fprints.htm.

Dictionary.com, s.v. "caution." Accessed March 24, 2016. http://www.dictionary.com/browse/caution>.

Design Observer. "Red Light, Green Light: The Invention of the Traffic Signal." http://designobserver.com/feature/red-light-green-light--the invention-of--the-traffic-signal/8627.

Fenelon, Francois. "Tell God." http://nhop.ca/tell-god-francois-fenelon.

Merriam-Webster.com, s.v. "decision." Accessed March 25, 2016.

A version of Joel's Joke. https://unijokes.com/joke-5580.

"Thought for Today." 2014. *Upper Room* (July/August): 66.

McClister, David. 2000. "The Scourging of Jesus." Truth Magazine 44 (January):11-12 http://www.truthmagazine.com/archives/volume44/v440106010.htm.

ABOUT THE AUTHOR

The author, Lesa McClain, has been a writer and lover of poetry for as long as she can remember. She became a novelist, as she says, "when God gave me this book."

She has been an employee of an automotive company for the past eighteen years as a process engineer and trainer. She is also a skilled mediator and has volunteered at a local mediation center, which she plans to resume after her retirement in about two years. She is also a part-time tax preparer working in the family tax preparation business.

She is a proud mother (to one daughter) and grandmother (to one three-year-old granddaughter) and enjoys spending time with them. She loves watching her granddaughter discover the world around her and expressing her independence.

She believes in creating a positive environment at home and at work. She also enjoys encouraging people of all ages to reach their potential, especially the younger generation who are just starting out. She has an encouraging word and a smile for everyone.

In her spare time, in addition to reading and writing poetry, she likes to read mystery thriller books, do crossword puzzles, and cook, always looking for a new dish to try.

Lesa attends New Prospect Missionary Church, Detroit, Michigan, and is a member of the Courtesy Ministry. She resides in Southfield, Michigan.